THE 21ST CENTURY LIKE THE 1ST

The REVIVAL of the THIRD DAY

DOMINIQUAE BIERMAN, PHD

THE REVIVAL OF THE THIRD DAY

THE REVIVAL OF THE THIRD DAY © 2016-2021 by Dominiquae Bierman

All rights reserved. This book may not be copied or reprinted for commercial gain or profit. The use of short quotations or occasional page copying for personal or group study is permitted and encouraged. Permission will be granted upon request. Reproduction can be permitted if officially requested to kad_esh_map@msn.com.

Unless otherwise identified, Scripture quotations are from: The King James Version or New American Standard Bible. Used by permission. All rights reserved.

Published by Zion's Gospel Press

52 Tuscan Way, Ste 202-412
St. Augustine, FL, 32092
shalom@zionsgospel.com

Paperback ISBN: 978-1-953502-53-7
E-Book ISBN: 978-1-953502-54-4

On occasion words such as Jesus, Christ, Lord and God have been changed by the author, back to their original Hebrew renderings, Yeshua, Messiah, Yahveh, and Elohim.

Bold or italicized emphasis or underlining within quotations is the author's own.

Printed in the United States of America

First Printing 2016, Second Printing June 2021

A Spiritual Earthquake

[Third Prediction: Death and Resurrection] Now, as Yeshua was going up to Jerusalem, He took the Twelve aside privately, and on the way He told them, "Look, we're going up to Jerusalem, and the Son of Man will be handed over to the ruling kohanim (priests) and Torah scholars. They will condemn Him to death and hand Him over to the Gentiles to mock, and to scourge, and to crucify. Yet on the third day, He will be raised up."
—Matthew 20: 17-19 TLV

On the third day, Esther put on her royal apparel and stood in the inner court of the palace in front of the king's hall. The king was sitting on his royal throne in the hall, facing the entrance. When the king saw Queen Esther standing in the courtyard, she found favor in his eyes, so the king held out to Esther the golden scepter in his hand, and Esther approached and touched the top of the scepter.
—Esther 5:1-2 TLV

Come, let us return to ADONAI. For He has torn, but He will heal us. He has smitten, but He will bind us up. After two days, He will revive us. On the third day, He will raise us up, and we will live in His presence. So let us know, let us strive to know ADONAI. Like dawn, His going forth is certain. He will come to us like the rain, like the latter rain watering the earth.
—Hosea 6:1-3 TLV

Contents

CHAPTER 1: The Prophecy of the Rose 1
The Prophecy of the Rose.............................. 1
The Azusa Revival Centennial 2
Revival Outside of the Camp – The Jerusa Revival 4

CHAPTER 2: Revival or Judgment on the Third Day?.... 7
The Key of Abraham 7
For 2 Days Yeshua Has Been Handed Over to the Gentiles ... 8

CHAPTER 3: How to Choose the Third Day Revival 13

CHAPTER 4: Uproot Replacement Theology! 19
Partaker Not Usurper! Not Replacer!.................... 21
The Menorah (7 Branch Lampstand) of Revival 21
The Third Watch of the Night........................... 22
Will You Watch from Midnight?........................ 25

APPENDIX 1: Two Weddings & One Divorce 27
The First Marriage 27
Prophetic Altar Call.................................... 33

APPENDIX 2: Revocation of the Council of Nicaea...... 35
Exposing the 23 Lies & Doctrinal Errors 37
Prayer Renouncing the First Council of Nicaea 41

APPENDIX 3: Connect With Us..................... 43
Other Books 43

Introduction

THE PROPHECY OF THE ROSE

*For where your treasure is,
there your heart will be also.*
—Matthew 6:21

DURING MY LAST RETREAT (Shabbat April 2, 2016) before the Second Act of Repentance at the Eastern Gates of America (Williamsburg-James-town), Yah showed me the dynamics of THE REVIVAL OF THE THIRD DAY. He has also shown me the importance of the Third Watch of the night starting at *midnight*; this watch is called *tikkun hazot* or the midnight watch.

The Prophecy of the Rose

When Yah gave me the Prophetic Word for the Church worldwide concerning *the rose* in 1993, He showed me the importance of restoring the Church to its Jewish roots and Hebrew foundations. He spoke to me on an El Al flight toward Tel Aviv from Zürich after my very first *Back to the Roots* conference in Herisau, Switzerland. There were many miracles and an awesome Glorious Outpouring. I was *awed* because the whole meeting was a meeting of Repentance from hatred of the Jews! I asked Abba, "Why is it so important to preach The Jewish roots to the Church?" He said, "It is a matter of *life and death*. The Church has been like a beautiful *rose* uprooted from her Garden and put in a vase of water for two days—but on the third day, if she is not replanted back, she will surely *die*!"

Out of that Prophecy came forth my book *The Healing Power of the Roots,* calling the church to *repentance* and to be re-grafted back into the Olive Tree of Israel, forsaking all replacement theology and Babylonian Christianity.

Many are healed, delivered, and transformed by reading this small, 70-page book and praying the prayers of repentance that break curses. This book is now available in many languages, including German, Spanish, Dutch, French, Norwegian, Finnish, Chinese, Italian, Estonian, Russian, and more languages to come. (Get the book: www.kad-esh.org and press on 'Shop.')

The Azusa Revival Centennial

In 2006 I was manning our booth with my husband and Team at the Azusa Revival Centennial celebrations in Los Angeles,

America. Two weeks before this conference, Abba notified me that we were to attend, and He sent us all the way from Jerusalem, Israel! With such short notice, we could not be featured in the Centennial Booklet, yet we had a booth all the way in the back that featured my books and Judaica. Prayer and worship formed a covering of angels over our booth and people of different denominations, including Lutherans and Methodists, were getting filled with the Spirit as they passed through our booth.

I will never forget a pastor's son who had bought my book *Grafted In*. He returned the next morning and gave us this testimony: "I have bought many different books in this convention, but it looks like I have wasted my money in vain, as the LORD is not letting me read anything except your book *Grafted In*!"

People were expectant for revival; there were many famous preachers! It was a great "happening," but revival did not "hit" at the Centennial Convention Center in Los Angeles. I saw the Angels of Revival all over the place with their arms crossed, *idle*, *bored*, and looking quite stern and serious! I asked Yah (God) why His Angels of Revival were *jobless*? His answer to me was the following:

There will be no revival without the central message that I have given you of repentance from replacement theology and restoration to the Jewish roots of the gospel! There will be no revival without Israel as center stage!

For if their (the Jews) rejection leads to the reconciliation of the world, what will their (the Jews) acceptance be but life from the dead?

—Romans 11:15 TLV

Life from the dead is revival! And it is brought forth by once again accepting the Jews with the Jewish roots of the faith! (Not religious Judaism, but the Hebrew foundations of the gospel!)

The Holy Spirit kept telling me:

If the Pentecostal-charismatic church stemming from the Azusa Street Revival does not repent of replacement theology, I will bypass them altogether!

Revival Outside of the Camp – The Jerusa Revival

Meanwhile, during the Centennial celebrations, we were invited to preach in the Filipino-American Missionary Alliance Church that had never enjoyed the Power of the Holy Spirit! No one was baptized in the Spirit or spoke in tongues in that church before we came!

The Pastor shared that they were praying "for God to have His way with them" and he was scared of what God was going to do, but he believed the appearance of these Israeli Jews was an answer to that prayer. I (Archbishop Dominiquae) grabbed the microphone (surprising the Pastor as he expected a man!) and said: "We are not from the Azusa Street Revival, neither from any known Christian denomination. We are Jews from Israel directly from *the Jerusalem* Revival that happened 2,000 years ago!" No one evangelized me. Yeshua came to speak to me at the Waters of the Sea of Galilee and told me: "*Run for your life, get baptized and get* saved!" Then I grabbed my guitar and began to sing my song "The Key of Abraham" that has become the Anthem of the MAP (Messianic Apostolic Prophetic) Revolution:

> Restore, restore the glory, that we lost so long ago. Make us one in You, Gentile and Jew.
> Together we'll arise and reach out to all the nations, as we are one in You, Gentile and Jew!
> For the Key of Abraham has been given to mankind, and the Key of Abraham opens all doors...
> It is time now to get rid of all the lies that separate us; it is time to know the truth and walk in love.
> Grafted in the Olive Tree, Israel both Jew and Gentile, reaching out to all the world with many signs...

As I was singing the song, our dancer team member began to twirl like a spinning top at the front of the church... Then a lady in the pew gave a loud scream and fell backward, she went to Heaven for four hours! Many of the people in the pews ran forward, repenting and falling under the Holy Spirit, then raised up praying in tongues for the first time! In the adjacent room the children were watching the happenings on a big screen, they began to repent for sin, rebellion, and disobedience to parents as they wept and ran into the sanctuary! All Heaven broke loose that day in that Missionary Alliance church. The

Pastor sat on the front pew with his eyes popping out of his eyelids amazed.... Four hours later, he sat next to me and asked me: "What happened Bishop Dominiquae?" The lady who had been taken to Heaven for four hours came back saying that Yeshua gave her a tour of Heaven and commanded her to *forgive*!

Chapter 2

REVIVAL OR JUDGMENT ON THE THIRD DAY?

The Key of Abraham

> *My desire is to bless those who bless you, but whoever curses you, I will curse, and in you, all the families of the earth will be blessed.*
> —Genesis 12:3 TLV

THE REVIVAL OF THE Third Day is the revival of *restoration* to the original foundations of faith with Israel. Yah (God) calls us to forsake all replacement theology with its pagan feasts and misinterpretations of the Holy Scriptures. He is calling us, once again, to adopt *the Jewish* apostles as the Church Fathers and the people of Israel as the Mother of the Nations!

THE REVIVAL OF THE THIRD DAY is the 21st century like the *first century*! THE REVIVAL OF THE THIRD DAY is returning to the roots of the gospel, forsaking the Gospel of Rome and returning to the Gospel made in Zion! The Gospel made in Zion is steeped in holiness, the Fear of YHVH (God), with signs, wonders, and miracles!

No other concocted "revival" by the works of the flesh will succeed or take root. For it is THE REVIVAL OF THE THIRD DAY, and it is like no other revival!

For 2 Days Yeshua Has Been Handed Over to the Gentiles

[Third Prediction: Death and Resurrection] Now as Yeshua was going up to Jerusalem, He took the Twelve aside privately; and on the way he told them, "Look, we're going up to Jerusalem, and the Son of Man will be handed over to the ruling kohanim (priests) and Torah scholars. They will condemn Him to death and hand Him over to the Gentiles to mock, and to scourge, and to crucify. Yet on the third day, He will be raised up."

—Matthew 20: 17-19 TLV

Yeshua, the Jewish Messiah has been handed over to the Gentiles to mock, scourge and crucify... for two days (two millennia!) Yeshua, the Jewish Messiah, has been mocked, scourged, and crucified afresh by a Church steeped in replacement theology and hatred for the Jews and everything Jewish.

His identity has been stolen, His name has been changed, and millions of His Jewish people are persecuted, humiliated, and murdered! All these things have happened in the name of Jesus Christ and for the sake of Christianity, born in Rome in the 4th century.

In the 4th century, through the Council of Nicaea, this replacement theology was established as church doctrine. The hatred of Jews, the Torah and everything Jewish, including the Birth and Eternal Name of the Messiah Yeshua, became church doctrine and maintains its power in many places and denominations! With each despised, humiliated, or murdered Jew, *it was Yeshua* that the Gentiles have persecuted! Yes, indeed Yeshua has been handed to the Gentiles for the last two days—two millennia of years!

But don't forget this one thing, loved ones, that with the LORD one day is like a thousand years, and a thousand years are like one day.

—2 Peter 3:8 TLV

"Yet on the third day, He will be raised up."

—Matthew 17:19

Yet in this 3rd millennium, He will be raised up as the Jewish Messiah that He is, as Yeshua, the King of the Jews! He is being raised up right now as Jews are being saved all over the world.

Yeshua is being raised up as Israel is restored to its Land and has managed to survive the hatred of the whole world and murderous spirit of all its Arab neighbors! Yeshua is *risen* as Israel is *risen*! It is the *acceptance* of the Jews (with Torah-with Jewish roots!) that brings life from the dead.

This acceptance brings revival to the very nations that have mocked, scourged, humiliated, and murdered Yeshua through every Jew that has been hated! With the pain of each life of millions of Jews, through sporadic persecution, crusades, Inquisitions (including the Spanish Inquisition), pogroms, the Shoa (Nazi Holocaust), Oslo Accords, false peace agreements, and BDS implemented mostly by the Christian church and recently by the Muslims as well, Yeshua experiences His pain afresh!

Whatever evil or good that has been done to the Jews is being done to *Yeshua*, the Savior, the Messiah and Anointed King of the Jews, the Son of YHVH (God) in the flesh... and He is ready to *judge* unless there is *repentance* and *restitution*!

And answering, the King will say to them, "Amen, I tell you, whatever you did to one of the least of these My brethren, you did it to Me." Then He will also say to those on the left, "Go away from Me, you cursed ones, into the everlasting fire which has been prepared for the devil and his angels. For I was hungry and you gave Me nothing to eat; I was thirsty and you gave Me nothing to drink; I was a stranger and you did not invite Me in; naked and you did not clothe Me; sick and in prison and you did not visit Me." Matthew 25: 41-43

The Brethren of Yeshua is the Nation of Israel, the Jewish people of today!

In order to overturn the judgment that the church and

the Nations deserve, *teshuva*—Repentance, returning for the purpose of *restoration* is needed!

We must choose both individually and nationally. Do we want the judgment of the Third Day or THE REVIVAL OF THE THIRD DAY?

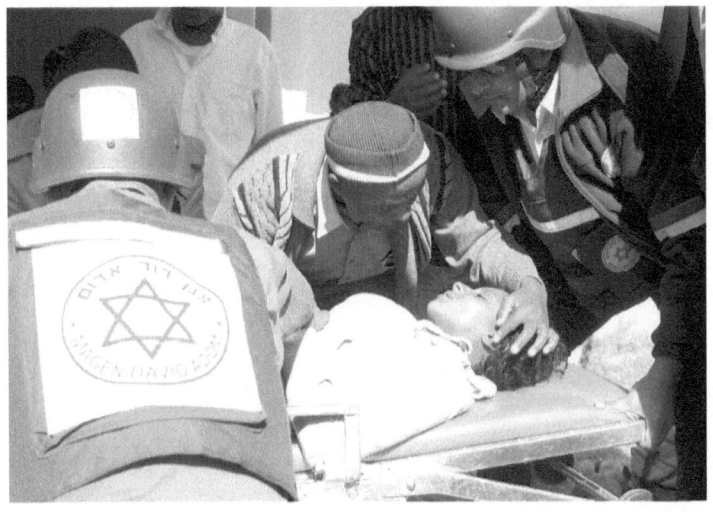

("Israeli Woman Injured after Rocket Attack | Flickr - Photo Sharing")[1]

---

1   "Israeli Woman Injured after Rocket Attack | Flickr - Photo Sharing" *Flickr.com*, All sizes | Israeli Woman Injured after Rocket Attack | Flickr - Photo Sharing!, 2013, www.flickr.com/photos/36313307@N06/3349396069/sizes/l/. Accessed 26 May 2021.

Chapter 3

HOW TO CHOOSE THE THIRD DAY REVIVAL

> *Adonai said to Moses, "Go to the people, and sanctify them today and tomorrow. Let them wash their clothing. Be ready for the third day. For on the third day Adonai will come down upon Mount Sinai in the sight of all the people."*
> —Exodus 19:10-11 TLV

WE MUST BE *SANCTIFIED* and *wash our clothing*. We must be *ready* for the Third Day Revival. This is the time to *prepare*! We must remember that *judgment* must first happen in the House of God. The Church is being *judged* before the world is, because "to whom much is given, much is required." We must *repent first*, and then the world will follow!

> For the time has come for judgment to begin with the house of God. If judgment begins with us first, what will be the end for those who disobey the Good News of God? 1 Peter 4:17 TLV

The time has come for judgment, and it starts with us first!

When My people, over whom My name is called, humble themselves and pray and seek My face and turn from their evil ways, then I will hear from heaven and will forgive their sin and will heal their land.

—2 Chronicles 7:14 TLV

- We must humble ourselves, pray, seek, and turn (teshuva-repentance)!
- We must be cleansed and wash our garments! He is coming for a Bride pure and holy!

Husbands love your wives just as Messiah also loved His community and gave Himself up for her to make her holy, having cleansed her by immersion in the Word.

Messiah did this so that He might present to Himself His glorious community (*Bride*)—not having stain or wrinkle or any such thing, but in order that she might be holy and blameless.

—Ephesians 5: 25-27

As a community, a Bride, or church, we must get rid of the stains and wrinkles in our Garment of Salvation! Yah (God) deals with us individually but also as a *community*, as a *body!* We need to get cleansed from all known sin of rebellion, disobedience, and unbelief, but we also need to get rid, as a *community* of believers, of all Doctrinal Lies and the major Doctrinal Lie is *replacement theology*! It is the Identity Theft of Messiah, His Name, His Feasts, and His Jewish people that has caused *the biggest stain* in the Garment of Salvation of the community of believers worldwide!

For THE REVIVAL OF THE THIRD DAY to occur, the community of believers in Messiah, world-wide, must *repent now* and forsake replacement theology in *all* its aspects! And there are many aspects of replacement theology! In fact, it is the Red Dragon of the Book of Revelation that persecutes the Woman (Israel) and her offspring!

Therefore rejoice, O heavens, and you who dwell in them! Woe to the earth and the sea, for the devil has come down to you with great rage, knowing that his time is short.

Now when the dragon saw that he had been thrown to the earth, he stalked the woman who had given birth to the male child. But the woman was given two wings of the great eagle so that she might fly away from the presence of the serpent into the wilderness, to the place where she is taken care of— for a time, times, and half a time.

—Revelation 12:12-14 TLV

This Red Dragon is sitting in the church through the Replaced Greek name of the Messiah, through pagan feasts, such as Christmas and Easter and Sunday worship, all that derived from Sun Worship. It is sitting in the Protestant church, the Evangelical church, the Pentecostal church, Charismatic church, the apostolic church and all denominations that are still attached with an umbilical cord to the Catholic church that calls itself the *mother*. That is why so many Evangelical leaders are *uniting* with the Pope and with the Catholic church. The Catholic church is still attached with the *umbilical cord* to *Rome* and not to Jerusalem. It is still attached to the false gospel preached by Eastern Roman Emperor Constantine, the Council of Nicaea and all Ecumenical Councils thereof.

We ought not, therefore, to have anything in common with the Jew, for the Savior has shown us another way; our worship following a more legitimate and more convenient course (the order of the days of the week). And consequently, in unanimously adopting this mode, we desire, dearest brethren, to separate ourselves from the detestable company of the Jew. (Excerpts from the Council of Nicaea 325 AD)

As long as the church calls the Jewish Messiah by its Greek Name and celebrates pagan-derived holidays stemming from Sun worship, it is attached to Rome and not to Jerusalem. It is attached to the Christmas Tree and not to the Olive Tree (Romans 11). It is attached to the Tree of Knowledge of religion and traditions of men, and not to the Tree of Life that is truth, who is Yeshua—the Jewish Messiah and the Word— the Torah made flesh that is true indeed! All things must be *restored* before Messiah's return to Jerusalem!

Repent, therefore, and return—so your sins might be blotted out, so times of relief might come from the presence of ADONAI and He might send Yeshua, the Messiah appointed for you. Heaven must receive Him until the time of the restoration of all the things that God spoke about long ago through the mouth of His holy prophets.

—Acts 3:19-21 TLV

Chapter 4

UPROOT REPLACEMENT THEOLOGY!

And said, "Truly I say to you, unless you are converted and become like children, you will not enter the kingdom of heaven."
—Matthew 18:3

REPLACEMENT THEOLOGY IS A demonic principality with many heads, and all the heads must be cut off in our spiritual lives, our worship and beliefs, if we are to be ready for the Revival of the Third Day!

In fact, most of the people in the different Messianic and Hebrew roots Movement are in confusion because they are adding "Jewish traditions" and "Hebrew understanding" on *unrepentant hearts.*

Replacement theology is *sneaky,* and it is not enough to

add *New Wine* into *old wine skins*. Repentance is needed in *all* denominations, including the Hebrew roots Movements that are in a terrible chaos trying to be "more Jewish than the Jews" and "more Hebrew than the Hebrews." Strife and arrogance are causing a Babylonian confusion!

The Third Day Revival is not exchanging one religious system for another one. It is not exchanging Christianity for Judaism! It is uprooting the tree of knowledge of religion and restoring the kingdom system of the tree of life!

Now concerning idol sacrifices, we know that we all have knowledge. Knowledge puffs up, but love builds up.

—1 Corinthians 8:1

We need to *repent* and become as little children with simple, child-like faith and obedience!

And said, "Truly I say to you, unless you are converted and become like children, you will not enter the kingdom of heaven."

—Matthew 18:3

So, get rid of all malice and all deceit and hypocrisy and envy and all *lashon hara* (slander, evil tongue, gossip). As newborn babes, long for pure spiritual milk, so that by it you may grow toward salvation—now that you have tasted that the Lord is good.

—1 Peter 2:1-3 TLV

When people *repent* of the fullness of replacement

theology in our meetings, their faces *shine* and many have given us this testimony:

"I feel born again, again!"

They become like *newborn babes* that now long for *pure spiritual milk*. That Milk that comes from the *rich root of the olive tree!*

If the first fruit is holy, so is the whole batch of dough; and if the root is holy, so are the branches. But if some of the branches were broken off and you—being a wild olive—were grafted in among them and became a partaker of the root of the olive tree with its richness, do not boast against the branches. But if you do boast, it is not you who supports the root, but the root supports you.

—Romans 11:16-18

Partaker, Not Usurper! Not Replacer!

The Third Day Revival calls us to return to Him, to Yeshua the Jewish Messiah, and to the love and *honor* of the Jewish people, the Israel of *Today*, who is the Mother of the Nations!

Yeshua is calling us to lay down our weapons, our lies and arrogances, to lay down all strife and seek Him. Only He can restore us as we *repent* from all personal sins and doctrinal lies. We *must seek Him*.

The Menorah (7 Branch Lampstand) of Revival

When My people, over whom My name is called, humble themselves and pray and seek My face and turn from their evil ways, then I will hear from heaven and will forgive their sin and will heal their land.
—2 Chronicles 7:14 TLV

1. Humility
2. Prayer
3. Seeking *Him*
4. Turning from active sin and sinful attitudes
5. Elohim hears
6. Elohim forgives
7. Elohim heals

The Third Watch of the Night

This is a very important strategy in order to prepare for the Third Day Revival!

The Third Watch of the night starts at *midnight* and ends at 3 AM!

The death of the firstborn in Egypt happens at *midnight,* the people of Israel *flee Egypt* on the Third Watch of the night!

So, it came about at midnight that ADONAI struck down all the firstborn in the land of Egypt, from the firstborn of Pharaoh sitting on his throne to the firstborn of the captive who was in the dungeon, and all the firstborn cattle.

Then Pharaoh rose up in the night, he and all his servants and all the Egyptians, and there was loud wailing in Egypt. For there was not a house where someone was not dead. So, he called for Moses and Aaron at night and said, "Rise up, go out from my people, both you and Bnei Yisrael, go, serve ADONAI as you have said. Take your flocks and your herds, as you said, and be gone! But bless me, too." Now the Egyptians urged the people, sending them out of the land quickly, for they thought, "We will all be dead!"
—Exodus 12:29-33

The church must flee replacement theology quickly! This is a matter of *life and death* as the Almighty spoke to me in 1993! If the church is not *replanted* back into the original Gospel made in Zion with Jewish roots she will die! There will be judgment instead of *revival*.

It is at *midnight* during the Third Watch of the night that Samson got *strength* to uproot the Gates of the Philistines and to escape their grip!

But Samson lay in bed till midnight, got up at midnight, grabbed the doors of the city gate along with the two gateposts, and pulled them up bar and all. Then he put them on his shoulders and carried them up to the top of the mountain that is near Hebron.
—Judges 16:3

At *midnight,* the Bridegroom comes!

But in the middle of the night, there was a shout, "Look, the bridegroom! Come out to meet him!" Then all those virgins got up and trimmed their lamps. Now the foolish ones said to the wise, "Give us some of your oil since our lamps are going out." But the wise ones replied, "No, there won't be enough for us and for you. Instead, go to those who sell, and buy some for yourselves."

—Matthew 25:6-9

At *midnight,* King David praised YHVH for His Torah and Commandments!

At midnight I rise to praise You, because of Your righteous rulings.

—Psalm 119:62

As Paul and Silas were doing the Third Watch at *midnight,* in jail, deliverance and revival hit the prison!

But about midnight, Paul and Silas were praying and singing hymns to God, and the prisoners were listening to them. Suddenly there was such a great earthquake that the foundations of the prison were shaken. Immediately all the doors were unlocked, and everyone's chains came loose.

—Acts 16:25-26

Notice that both the Apostles chains fell but also *all the other prisoners were delivered,* Haleluyah! That is the power of the Third Watch or the Midnight Watch!

Right afterward, the jailer and his family got saved! Now that is *true revival*!

The jailer called for lights and rushed in; and trembling with fear, he fell down before Paul and Silas. After he brought them out, he said, "Sirs, what must I do to be saved?"

They said, "Put your trust in the Lord Yeshua and you will be saved—you and your household!"

Then they spoke the Word of the Lord to him, along with everyone in his household. He took them that very hour and washed their wounds, and at once he was immersed—he and all his household. The jailer brought them to his house and set food before them, and he was overjoyed that he with his entire household had put their trust in God.

—Acts 16:29-32

Will You Watch from Midnight?

We in Kad-Esh MAP Ministries have decided to obey the prompting of the Holy Spirit and set aside, separate, and consecrate the *Third Watch of the Night* starting at *midnight* as the strategy for preparing for the Third Day Revival that has been promised! Since people are scattered all over the world, whenever someone prays at midnight, it covers another hour around the Globe, until the whole Globe will be covered with praise and prayer at *midnight,* somewhere!

We invite you to choose one day or a few days a week as your *midnight* watch! You can do it alone or in *community*, which is more powerful! You can do it in central locations or prayer meetings on the *internet*!

We will assign some team members of Kad-Esh MAP Ministries to lead once a week a midnight watch through the internet covering each day (beginning at midnight where that team member resides). Our website will list these Midnight Watches so anyone that desires to join through internet can pray together with our team.

The major thrust is to *praise* Him like King David, Paul, and Silas. Then offer prayer and praise Him for the following (and as He leads):

- Entreating YHVH for THE REVIVAL OF THE THIRD DAY
- Praying for the Bride of Messiah to be completely Free from replacement theology
- Praying for the deliverance, salvation, and restoration of Israel
- Praying for the salvation of your nation
- Praying for all leaders and rulers in government
- Praying for church/congregations and ministry leaders
- Praying for whatever the Holy Spirit will impress
- Praising Him for His righteous rules to prevail!

Also pray for us as we move forward into THE REVIVAL OF THE THIRD DAY! Pray that Elohim will give us boldness, utterance, strength, health, unity in the Team, and provision to bring the Gospel made in Zion to all the nations of the world!

For His glory alone!

The spiritual earthquake has begun!

Archbishop Dominiquae Bierman

"For Zion's sake I will not keep silent."

—Isaiah 62:1

Appendix 1

TWO WEDDINGS & ONE DIVORCE

The First Marriage

THE FOLLOWING ILLUSTRATION WILL explain why Christianity was 'the womb' of the Spanish Inquisition, the Crusades, and the Nazi Holocaust. Yahveh-God is looking to the church for repentance in order to influence the nations and fulfill the mandate of Matthew 28:19 *"Go and make disciples of all nations."*

The first and original church was married to a Jewish Husband by the name of Yeshua the Messiah & into His family the Jewish people (Ephesians 2:14 and Romans 11). The Wedding Ceremony took place in Jerusalem. It was ratified and sealed by the spilling of the blood of the Husband and by the breaking of His body. (Luke 22:15–20) The time of this marriage was the holy biblical Feast of Passover. The fruit of this miraculous wedding was thousands and thousands of people, both Jews and Gentiles, saved and healed. Even the shadow of this holy bride healed the sick, as signs and wonders and miracles followed her wherever she went in the name of her Husband Yeshua.

This marriage led the wife to much suffering. Many in the world did not love her Husband and tried to kill her by persecuting her and even throwing her to the lions during the Roman Empire's reign of terror. Those were hard years. After many years of suffering, Yeshua's wife had become weary. He had gone to prepare a place for her and had not come back yet.

She started to get tired from her lifestyle as an outcast, persecuted and hunted at every corner. She longed for peace at any price. She longed for the warm embrace of a Husband who would provide her with peace and security here on this earth... At her weakest point an earthly king appeared. (Matthew 10:34, John 14:27, Jeremiah 8:11)

This earthly king was influential and powerful by earthly standards. He could stop the killing and persecution against her. He could give her the security she longed for... *If* only she would agree to divorce this Jewish Husband of hers and completely separate from His family Israel, and from that Book that she treasured so much – where He had left her all of His instructions and the family legacy of God's Word.

This powerful king seemed to be a spiritual man. He claimed that her Jewish Husband had appeared to him in a dream and had given him the crown of the Roman Empire. His deceptive charm and appeasing manners managed to attract the very weary bride of Messiah, but not all were deceived. There was a portion of the bride/church/ecclesia that was not fooled by the charms of this deceitful king. These were the Messianic Jews of the time.

They were too rooted in the writings of the Holy Book and the ancient Hebrew Scriptures to be deceived. But the vast majority of the believers at that time were Gentiles, and they did not want any more suffering on behalf of the Book, its Author, or His family.

They wanted freedom and peace at all cost.

The powerful Constantine sang the song of peace and safety and prepared a bed of roses... The Gentile portion of the church slept with him, falling into violent adultery and wounding the heart of her heavenly Jewish Husband. In order to appease the conscience of this adulterous church, Constantine decided to legalize this unholy union in the year AD 325 by means of a wedding ceremony called the Council of Nicaea and drawing up an ungodly and illegal marriage contract called the Nicean Creed.

He used his worldly power to draw all the gentile church fathers, which for the most part were already anti-Semitic and hated their Jewish roots. These church fathers were to be witnesses of this horrendous divorce and the adulterous new marriage between the predominantly Gentile church and another Jesus, a product of Constantine's own creation.

This alternative Savior came with another family, another book (totally disconnected from the ancient Hebrew writings), other customs, Laws, festivals, traditions and ways of measuring time.

Knowing that his brand-new wife was accustomed to worshipping God, he organized for her a god that would suit her perfectly by not demanding any holiness from her. He presented a god of peace that was lenient towards a mixture of paganism and holiness: An all-inclusive god, who accepted all traditions and blended them into one.

Now Passover and First Fruits, the festival of Yeshua's resurrection, would become The Feast of Ishtar, the goddess of fertility, or Easter with bunny rabbits and Easter eggs. (At that time eggs were dipped in the blood of the babies sacrificed to the goddess, thus the tradition of painting the eggs).

Now the fay of worship would change from Shabbat to Sunday in order to eternalize the sun god who for now would be called Jesus – yet it was another Jesus and certainly not Yeshua, the Jewish Messiah.

Then the day of the winter solstice of witchcraft, called Saturnalia or Paganalia, celebrated on the 25th of December in the Roman Empire, was to acquire the name Christmas and would celebrate the birth of this false Messiah. For the true Messiah was born during the holy biblical Feast of Tabernacles and followed the Hebrew biblical calendar, not the Roman one. (Daniel 7:25-27, Jeremiah 10:2-4 about the Christmas tree.)

The ancient Holy Book of the Hebrew Scriptures was to become obsolete, and its Laws done away with. Instead, Constantine compiled the apostolic writings, the letters of Paul and others into a new holy book and called it the New Testament. He gave this holy book his own perverse interpretation, completely divorced from the foundational Hebrew Writings whom he and his followers called the 'Old Testament.' (Matthew 5:17–21)

"In rejecting their custom, we may transmit to our descendants the legitimate way of celebrating Easter... We ought not therefore to have anything in common with the Jew, for the Savior has shown us another way; our worship following a more legitimate and more convenient course (the order of the days of the week); And consequently, in unanimously adopting this mode, we desire dearest brethren to separate ourselves from the detestable company of the Jew." (Excerpt from *The Nicene Creed*, year 325, found in *Eusebius, Vita Const. Lib III 18-20)*

This creed and its instructions are still followed by most Christians today with the celebration of Easter, Christmas, Sunday (replacing Shabbat), and the rejection of the Laws of God.

Indeed, a new religion had been born. It had a gentile god by the name of Jesus Christ, an apostle by the name of Constantine, a new book by the name of the New Testament (although compiled from the apostolic writings, which are completely Yah-inspired, it was deceitfully interpreted through gentile eyes and gentile theologians), and new traditions, and unholy festivals such as Easter, Christmas, Sunday, and Halloween.

And most importantly... *no Jews*... no, not even the Messiah.

What has been the fruit of this adulterous marriage?

Either make the tree good and its fruit good, or else make the tree bad and its fruit bad; for a tree is known by its fruit.

—Matthew 12:33

The fruit of the first holy matrimony were salvations and healings. The fruit of this ungodly and pagan marriage were forced conversions and killings, yes even mass destructions of the family of Yeshua the Messiah, (the true Husband), in the name of the false Jesus Christ god created by Constantine.

A god who, according to Constantine in the Nicene Creed, had shown us *another way*. What was that way? It is a way of jealousy, hatred, killing, destruction, and Lawlessness. Horrendous Christian events such as pogroms, the holy inquisition, and the holocaust, have taken place since this ungodly 4th century marriage and the creation of this false religion.

The hatred conveyed in the Nicene Creed against the Jews and anything Jewish, including the Torah and the Old Testament, has continued through the great Protestant Reformation of the 16th century, and it still influences Christians today.

The following excerpt is from *Our Hands are Stained with Blood* by Michael Brown, as he quotes directly from Martin Luther's writings.

Luther wrote this after he was frustrated from trying to

evangelize the Jews and when he was old and sick:

"What shall we Christians do with this damned rejected race of Jews? First, their synagogues should be set on fire. Secondly, their homes should likewise be broken down and destroyed. Thirdly, they should be deprived of their prayer books and Talmud's. Fourthly, their rabbis must be forbidden under threat of death to teach anymore. Fifthly, passports and traveling privileges should be absolutely forbidden to the Jews... To sum up dear princes and nobles, who have Jews in your domains, if this advice of mine does not suit you, then find a better one. So that you and we may all be free of this insufferable, devilish burden – the Jews."
(Luther and Brown)

Hitler followed Luther's instructions meticulously and quoted him while doing so. The fruit? Over six million Jews exterminated in horrendous death camps and gas chambers, and many survivors scarred for life.

Prophetic Altar Call

After two days He will revive us; on the third day He will raise us up, that we may live in His sight. Let us know; let us pursue the knowledge of Yahveh. His going forth is established as the morning; He will come to us like the rain, like the latter and former rain to the earth.

—Hosea 6:2–3

The Third Day is upon us, the Third Millennium, and this is the Father's call to His Third Day church:

Come let us return to Yeshua, to our Jewish Messiah, His Jewish family and His ancient Hebrew Scriptures. Come let us reinterpret the New Testament through the eyes of the holy Scriptures. Let us separate ourselves from our pagan husband, Constantine, and his false Jesus and let us go back to the true Messiah Yeshua, to His Father's Laws and Precepts, to true divine holy grace, to true love and holiness. Let us return to Jerusalem, and let us be made whole from centuries of adultery and paganism, as we go back to the original apostolic Jewish roots of our faith.

In Yeshua's love and brokenness;
Archbishop Dr. Dominiquae & Rabbi Baruch Bierman

Disclaimer: What this Article is Not Saying

- It is *not* saying to go back to the laws of Rabbinic Judaism.
- It is *not* implying that all Christians have anti-Semitism.
- It is *not* disqualifying the countless believers who call on the name of Jesus Christ meaning the *true* Jewish Messiah Yeshua.
- It is *not* disqualifying worship on Sunday, Monday, Tuesday or any other day.
- It is *not* disqualifying the New Testament as Bible (Only the wrong, 'divorced' interpretations of it).

Appendix 1

REVOCATION OF THE COUNCIL OF NICAEA

FROM THE LETTER OF the Emperor (Constantine) to all those not present at the council. (Found in Eusebius, Vita Const.,Lib III 18-20)

When the question relative to the sacred festival of Easter arose, it was universally thought that it would be convenient that all should keep the feast on one day; for what could be more beautiful and more desirable than to see this festival, through which we receive the hope of immortality, celebrated by all with one accord and in the same manner? It was declared to be particularly unworthy for this, the holiest of festivals, to follow the customs (the calculation) of the Jews who had soiled their hands with the most fearful of crimes, and whose minds were blinded. In rejecting their custom we may transmit to our descendants the legitimate mode of celebrating Easter; which we have observed from the time of the Saviour's passion (according to the day of the week).

We ought not, therefore, to have anything in common with the Jew, for the Saviour has shown us another way; our worship following a more legitimate and more convenient course (the order of the days of the week: And consequently in unanimously adopting this mode, we desire, dearest brethren to separate ourselves from the detestable company of the Jew. For it is truly shameful for us to hear them boast that without their direction, we could not keep this feast. How can they be in the right, they who, after the death of the Saviour, have no longer been led by reason but by wild violence, as their delusion may urge them? They do not possess the truth in this Easter question, for in their blindness and repugnance to all improvements they frequently celebrate two Passovers in the same year. We could not imitate those who are openly in error.

How, then, could we follow these Jews who are most certainly blinded by error? For to celebrate a Passover twice in one year, is totally inadmissible.

But even if this were not so it would still be your duty not to tarnish your soul by communication with such wicked people (the Jews). You should consider not only that the number of churches in these provinces make a majority, but also that it is right to demand what our reason approves, and that we should have nothing in common with the Jews. (Gleaned from Dr. Henry R. Percival's *"The Nicaean and Post Nicaean Fathers."* Vol. XIV Grand Rapid: Erdmans pub. 1979, pgs. 54-55)

Exposing the 23 Lies & Doctrinal Errors

1. "When the question relative to the sacred festival of Easter..."

    The truth: sacred to pagan traditions, this is a pagan name derived from the goddess Ishtar. (Exodus 20:3, Hosea 2:17)

2. "...arose, it was universally..."

    The truth: Everyone in the universe? Is Constantine the king of the universe? (Isaiah 14:3)

3. "...thought that it would be convenient..."

    The truth: God does not call us to convenience but obedience. (John 15:10)

4. "...that all should keep the feast on one day; for what could be more beautiful and more desirable than to see this festival, through which we receive the hope of immortality, celebrated by all with one accord and in the same manner?...."

    The truth: Without Jews? John 17:21, unity between Jew and Gentile brings the salvation of all mankind. (Psalms 133 and Isaiah 56)

5. "...It was declared to be particularly unworthy..."

    The truth: Yahveh's choice of dates is "unworthy" to Constantine as he sets himself above God's choosing of timings. (Daniel 7:25 and Isaiah 14:13 [Lucifer])

6. "...for this, the holiest of festivals to follow the customs (the calculation) of the Jews..."

The truth: Which are the original and true calculations? (Leviticus 23:1, Jeremiah 31:31–34)

7. "...who had soiled their hands with the most fearful of crimes, and whose minds were blinded..."

The truth: In John 10:17–18 Yeshua lays His own life down (See also John 3:16.) the accusation that "The Jews killed Christ" has been the incentive for the extermination of millions of Jews from that point onwards and until this day, including the Holocaust. (See Matthew 7:17–20, the fruit of this theology)

8. "...In rejecting their custom..."

The truth: God's custom according to His Word.

9. "...we may transmit to our descendants the legitimate..."

The truth: according to Constantine but not according to the Word of God. (Matthew 26:2, Leviticus 23:1–4, Genesis 1:14, John 20:1–9, Matthew 12:39)

10. "...mode of celebrating Easter which we have observed..."

The truth: pagan name and feast not mentioned in the Holy Scriptures.

11. "We ought not therefore to have anything in common with the Jew, for the Savior has shown us another way"

The truth: Yeshua is Jewish, so if nothing is in common with the Jews, nothing is in common with the Messiah. (Matthew 1, John 19;19, Luke 1:59, Luke 2:21)

12. "our worship following a more legitimate and more convenient course, the order of the days of the week"

The truth: Constantine legitimizes his own ideas in order to gain political power and control and he attempts to dethrone the Word of God on this subject – setting himself and his opinions above Yah and His unchanging Word.

13. "...And consequently in unanimously..."

The truth: without the Jews from which salvation comes! (John 4:22)

14. "...adopting this mode, we desire, dearest brethren to separate ourselves from the detestable company of the Jew For it is truly shameful for us to hear them boast that without their direction we could not keep this feast. How can they be in the right, they who, after the death of the Savior..."

The truth: Romans 11:15–20 warns the Gentiles not to be arrogant against the Jews or Gentiles will be cut of the Olive tree!

15. "...have no longer been led by reason..."

The truth: True sons of God are not led by reason or Greek philosophy but by the Spirit of God. Since Constantine and the Council of Nicaea, the church in its vast majority has been led by reason and by theologians instead of by powerful apostles. (Romans 8:14, Ephesians 2:20) – these are all Jewish.

16. "but by wild violence, as their delusion may urge them"

The truth: What wild violence is he talking about? Unsupported accusation used many times to incite the masses against the Jews like in the Protocols of the Elders of Zion?

17. "They do not possess the truth in this Easter question, for in their blindness and [15th lie] repugnance to all improvements"

The truth: traditions of demons and men that make null and void the Word of God (Matthew 15:3,4, Mark 7:13)

18. "They frequently celebrate two Passovers in the same year. We could not imitate those who are openly in error. How, then, could we follow these Jews who are most certainly blinded by error?"

The truth: Is following the biblical customs error? Who is really blinded here? Gentiles are supposed to be grafted into Israel's Olive tree and not vice versa! (Romans 11:15–20)

19. "For to celebrate a Passover twice in one year is totally inadmissible."

The truth: 2 Chronicles 30:1–3, it is totally scriptural.

20. "But even if this were not so it would still be your duty not to tarnish your soul by communication with such wicked people (the Jews)."

The truth: In other words, Constantine's purpose is to separate from the Jews and the Torah no matter what! Why? 1 John 4:1–3 states that the spirit of anti-Messiah, in operation through Constantine, removes the identity of Messiah as a Jew, and sets himself above God and His Word and His sovereign choice of choosing the Jews to bring salvation.

21. "You should consider not only that the number of churches in these provinces make a majority"

The truth: God has never worked with "majorities" but with obedience. Trusting in the arm of the flesh or the opinions of men brings about a curse! (Deuteronomy 28:1–14, Jeremiah 17:5, Judges 7:2–8, 1 Samuel 14:6)

22. "...but also that it is right to demand what our reason approves..."

The truth: Human reasoning? (1 Corinthians 1:27, Isaiah 29:14b)

23. "...and that we should have nothing in common with the Jews."

The truth: or with the Jewish Messiah or His salvation – John 4:22, Romans 11:15–20. He set the Gentile part of the church onto a path of self-destruction, remaining a wild olive instead of being grafted into the cultivated Olive tree – which is Israel – because of arrogance, removing the foundations of the Jewish apostles and prophets. (Psalms 11:3, Ephesians 2:20, Revelation 21:14)

Prayer Renouncing the First Council of Nicaea

Please pray. You can copy and pass it on, and please let us know of your decision.

Before the Almighty God of Israel, I stand and hereby renounce the First Council of Nicaea as led by Constantine. I renounce its foundation and all the anti-Jewish fruit that came out of it. I renounce every doctrinal error and every lie in it, including replacement theology in all of its aspects.

I hereby affirm my faith in Yahveh, the God of Israel, who is the Creator of the Universe and my Father through the atoning death of His Holy Son Yeshua, who is both the promised Jewish Messiah and God in the flesh. I hereby affirm my faith in the resurrection of Yeshua the Messiah and the outpouring of the Holy Spirit of God from the Day of Shavuot (Pentecost) and onwards, to all that repent and believe in the Son. I hereby affirm my belief that I am grafted into the Olive Tree that represents Israel, and together with the believing Jewish people, I will inherit eternal life. I hereby affirm that the God of Israel will never forsake His people, neither will He forget His covenant with the Jews or with the Ecclesia (Called out Ones - Church).

I thank you, Holy Father, for removing all the curses that have come into my life and into my nation due to our belief in the tenets of faith stated in the Council of Nicaea concerning the Jews and the Jewish foundations of the faith. I beg you and thank you for pouring out your great mercy and forgiveness over myself, my family, and my nation. I hereby commit myself to walk in truth as You reveal it to me and in love with all my fellow men and especially my (and the Church's) spiritual parents, the Jewish people, according to Genesis 12:1-3.

Appendix 3

CONNECT WITH US

Other Books

Order now online: www.kad-esh.org/shop/

The MAP Revolution (Free E-Book)
Find Out Why Revival Does Not Come... Yet!

The Identity Theft
The Return of the 1st Century Messiah

From Sickology to a Healthy Logic
The Product of 18 Years Walking Through Psychiatric Hospitals

ATG: Addicts Turning to God
The Biblical Way to Handle Addicts and Addictions

The Healing Power of the Roots
It's a Matter of Life or Death!

Grafted In
It's Time to Take the Nation's!

Sheep Nations
It's Time to Take the Nations!

Restoring the Glory: The Original Way
The Ancient Paths Rediscovered

Stormy Weather
Judgment Has Already Begun, Revival is Knocking at the Door

Yeshua is the Name
The Important Restoration of the Original Hebrew Name of the Messiah

Defeating Depression
This Book is a Kiss from Heaven!

The Key of Abraham
The Blessing or the Curse?

Yes!
The Dramatic Salvation of Archbishop Dr. Dominiquae Bierman

Eradicating the Cancer of Religion
Hint: All People Have It

Restoration of Holy Giving
Releasing the True 1,000 Fold Blessing

Connect With Us

Vision Negev
The Awesome Restoration of the Sephardic Jews

The Woman Factor by Rabbi Baruch Bierman
Freedom From Womanphobia

The Bible Cure for Africa & the Nations
Turn the Key of Abraham into
the Blessing Position for Africa!

Music Albums
www.kad-esh.org/shop/

The Key of Abraham

Abba Shebashamayim

Uru

Retorno

Get Equipped & Partner with Us

Global Revival MAP (GRM) Israeli Bible School
Take the most comprehensive video Bible school online that focuses on dismantling replacement theology.
For more information or to order, please contact us:

www.grmbibleschool.com

grm@dominiquaebierman.com

United Nations for Israel Movement
We invite you to join us as a member and partner with $25 a month, which supports the advancing of this End time vision that will bring true unity to the body of the Messiah. We will

see the One New Man form, witness the restoration of Israel, and take part in the birthing of SHEEP NATIONS. Today is an exciting time to be serving Him!

www.unitednationsforisrael.org

info@unitednationsforisrael.org

Global Re-Education Initiative (GRI) Against Anti-Semitism

Discover the Jewishness of Jesus and defeat Christian anti-Semitism with this online video course to see revival in your nation!

www.against-antisemitism.com

info@against-antisemitism.com

Join Our Annual Israel Tours

Travel through the Holy Land and watch the Hebrew Holy Scriptures come alive.

www.kad-esh.org/tours-and-events/

To Send Offerings to Support our Work

Your help keeps this mission of restoration going far and wide.

www.kad-esh.org/donations

CONTACT US

Archbishop Dr. Dominiquae & Rabbi Baruch Bierman

Kad-Esh MAP Ministries | www.kad-esh.org

info@kad-esh.org

Connect With Us

United Nations for Israel | www.unitednationsforisrael.org

info@unitednationsforisrael.org

Zion's Gospel Press | shalom@zionsgospel.com

52 Tuscan Way, Ste 202-412, 32092 St. Augustine Florida, USA

+1-972-301-7087

www.ingramcontent.com/pod-product-compliance
Lightning Source LLC
Chambersburg PA
CBHW022231080526
44577CB00005B/180